759 `06

Church of Ireland College of Education
LIBRARY

All loans must be returned by the latest date below. Failure to do so may incur suspension of borrowing rights.

William Orpen
1878 - 1931

BRUCE ARNOLD

TOWN HOUSE, DUBLIN
IN ASSOCIATION WITH
THE NATIONAL GALLERY OF IRELAND

Published in 1991 by

Town House

41 Marlborough Road

Donnybrook

Dublin 4

in association with The National Gallery of Ireland

British Library Cataloguing in Publication Data

Arnold, Bruce

William Orpen.—(Lives of Irish artists)

1. Ireland. Paintings

I. Title II. Orpen, Sir William 1878-1931

III. National Gallery of Ireland

759.2915

ISBN: 0-948524-25-1

Cover: *A Woman* (1906)

Title page: *Self Portrait* (1899)

Managing editor: Treasa Coady

Series editor: Brian P Kennedy (NGI)

Text editor: Elaine Campion

Design concept: Q Design

Typeset by Printset & Design Ltd, Dublin

Printed in Italy

CONTENTS

Bruce Arnold is literary editor of the *Irish Independent*, and author of the definitive life of William Orpen, entitled *Orpen: Mirror to an Age*. He has written four novels, *A Concise History of Irish Art*, books about Irish politics in the 1970s, and about Margaret Thatcher. He recently published *An Art Atlas of Britain and Ireland*.

William Orpen had perhaps a greater influence on Irish art in the twentieth century than any other painter. It was an influence which he achieved through teaching. He took and moulded a generation of students, at the Metropolitan School of Art in Dublin, during the period from 1900 up to the First World War, and then saw them become the artists and teachers of succeeding generations. Seán Keating, Patrick Tuohy, Leo Whelan, Margaret Clarke, Beatrice Glenavy, even Mainie Jellett, were all products, in whole or in part, of an art education which had been re-shaped and revitalised by Orpen.

In its turn, that next generation taught Orpen's principles, and nurtured a style which remained in vogue from the 1920s to the 1950s, and would be proudly acknowledged today by Thomas Ryan, the president of the Royal Hibernian Academy, and by many of his colleagues there. In the best sense, more than half a century after his death at the age of fifty-three, in 1931, Orpen's code of practice could be summed up by the advice of architect Christopher Wren for any visitor to St Paul's Cathedral:

Si monumentum requiris, circumspice (If you seek a monument to him, look around you).

'Orpen as Teacher' is only one aspect of this great artist. He was also among the most successful portrait painters of this century. He was deeply affected by the tragedy of trench warfare in the First World War, and from the experience he became a war artist of considerable impact on his era and on posterity. He was masterly in the way he drew and painted the nude. He was as subtle and varied in self-portraiture as any painter since Rembrandt. And with all of this, he was also a witty, delightful, complicated, lovable, and in the end tragic human being.

Essentially he was torn between two quite different views of himself and of art. His love of Ireland provided him with an excuse for fun and an indulgence in triviality. The story is told of him walking down a Dublin street in the company of serious men of art. A group of ragged children passed them, kicking a tin along in the gutter. Suddenly Orpen left his rather pompous companions and set off in hasty pursuit, joining in the urchins' games, laughing and shouting down the street, totally lost in the escapism they provided. Dublin offered that kind of release to him, from the burden of fame and fortune in London, the problems of wealth, and the boredom of a succession of well-paid portrait commissions. Consequently, when he came back to Ireland on holidays, or to teach at the Metropolitan Art School, he behaved irreverently, poking fun at the literary revival, mocking writers like Yeats, teasing the academicians, misbehaving and getting drunk. His best friends were men who were equally irreverent, such as George Moore and Hugh Lane. They all suffered for it, and could only take the high seriousness of Dublin's cultural life if they also mocked it. And they did this with wit and enthusiasm.

Yet it was as a teacher that he made his greatest impact, and for Ireland this is where a substantial part of his appeal lies. He learned and then taught the finest principles of practical draughtsmanship and good painting technique, and he passed them on to anyone willing to learn. He scorned the faint-hearted. If you wanted to paint, he believed, you gave it everything. Your starting point was clear and precise draughtsmanship, to which a painstaking understanding of colour and its rules was then added, with compositional skills, a sense of rhythm and movement, and originality of concept.

BACKGROUND AND EDUCATION

Born in 1878, the youngest of a family of five, William Newenham Montague Orpen was destined to be a painter. He drew pictures from early childhood, and he was accomplished enough, both with pencil and with paints, at the age of ten to impress his mother with the inevitability of sending him to one of the two art schools then in Dublin.

It was an unusual decision. Orpen's father and grandfather were successful lawyers, with a law practice which comfortably absorbed two of his brothers and his brother-in-law, and to this day exists with Orpen descendants working in it. But his mother, a Caulfeild, was of a creative disposition, and indulged this leaning in her insistence that the youngest in the family should pursue an artistic life.

Orpen was within six weeks of his thirteenth birthday when he went to the Metropolitan School of Art, in the autumn of 1891. For six years he triumphed there, winning every possible honour, including gold medals, against art students from all over the British Isles. It was a firm grounding, often overlooked in favour of the impact which the Slade School of Art in London had when he moved there, in the autumn of 1898. Again, he became the leading figure, outstripping painters such as Augustus John, and finishing his time with the outstanding early canvas, *The Play Scene from 'Hamlet'*, in which he included many of his friends and fellow-students.

12

ə♦

THE EARLY WORKS

The dominant movement in art at the time in England found expression through the New English Art Club. William Rothenstein, Charles Conder, Augustus John, Philip Wilson Steer and Henry Tonks (both of whom had taught Orpen at the Slade), Ambrose McEvoy, Michel Salaman and Herbert Everett were exhibitors or associates, and formed, though only loosely, a 'school' which had derived, in its early days, from the impact on English art of James McNeill Whistler. Their lives centred mainly on the area around the Slade, particularly Fitzroy Street, and the studios and

cont. p25

ILLUSTRATIONS

PLATE 1

The Mirror 1900

PLATE 2

The Bedroom 1900

14

Pl 1 Emily Scobel, Orpen's model for this and several other works, was part of the Fitzroy Street set, and went to Normandy with Orpen and Albert Rutherston in the summer of 1900. Orpen wanted to marry her, but she refused. She considered him 'too ambitious'. The painting was inspired by seventeenth-century Dutch interiors, small-scale portraits, and by the work of Whistler. It draws unashamedly from his portraits of his mother, and of the historian Carlyle.

Oil on canvas; 50.8 x 40.6 cm
Tate Gallery, London

Pl 2   T*his work, painted in Normandy, shows a small bedroom in the hotel in Cany, with Emily Scobel as Orpen's model. He was greatly attracted by the subdued eroticism of such subjects; he loved the four-poster, the tester-bed, and the Empire-period bed shown in this work, because of the way in which the drapes and furnishings created a warm, womb-like atmosphere. Again, the influence is partly seventeenth-century Dutch, delicately realised interiors, full of benign tension and human appeal.*

Oil on canvas; 53.9 x 60.9 cm
Private collection

15

Pl 3   T*hough Augustus John is said to have disliked this profoundly revealing presentation of his bohemian character, his reasons are more likely to have been jealousy than an objective criticism. This was the kind of full-length portrait which brought Orpen the attention and the commissions on which his life's work was based. The setting has the sombre realism of Orpen's work at the beginning of the century.*

Oil on canvas; 99 x 93.9 cm
National Portrait Gallery, London

PLATE 3

Augustus John 1900

16

Pl 4   **O**rpen's early influences were dictated, to an extent,
by the magnificent series of exhibitions at the Royal
Academy, London, and also at the Guildhall. But in 1904
he went with the art dealer Hugh Lane to Madrid, and
was captivated by the paintings he saw in the Prado,
especially those by Velázquez. At the time, too, he found
one of his finest models, Lottie Stafford, a washerwoman

PLATE 4

The Wash House 1905

from Chelsea, the model for this and other masterpieces.

Oil on canvas; 91.4 x 96.5 cm
National Gallery of Ireland

PLATE 5

A Woman 1906

18

Pl 5 **O**rpen found this a troublesome and difficult work. *At one stage his father called to see the painting and was embarrassed at its frankness. It is one of the great English nudes of the twentieth century, and a much prized possession of the Leeds City Art Gallery. Its original owner, Sam Wilson, also bought* The Red Scarf, *a fine early portrait of Orpen's wife, with many of the inspirations from Spanish art.*

Oil on canvas; 57.1 x 81.2 cm
Leeds City Art Galleries

PLATE 6

Mrs St George 1912

19

Pl 6

20

Evelyn St George was the wife of an Irish land agent. She and Orpen had an affair which began in about 1908 and lasted until the middle of the First World War. She had an enormous influence on his art, pushing him towards a sense of his own greatness, and making him paint works which were grand in concept and inspired in technique and originality. His standing portrait of her was undertaken with the intention of not using primary colours.

Oil on canvas; 213.3 x 91.4 cm
Private collection

Pl 7

Orpen met and fell in love with Yvonne Aubicq during the First World War. His first paintings of her were wartime propaganda works. After the war he painted several works with her as model, among them two masterpieces of British art. Early Morning *was a severe test of Orpen's view that a nude has to be also a person, and therefore a portrait. He instils his subject with real character, and achieves a tremendous result.*

Oil on canvas; 90.1 x 85 cm
Private collection

(Photo courtesy of Sotheby's)

PLATE 7

Early Morning 1922

PLATE 8

Sunlight *c* 1925

22

Pl 8   This *painting, which dates from the mid-1920s, was completed in Orpen's studio. On the wall is his Monet, part of his collection, representing his success and wealth. Clients for portraits queued at his studio in Chelsea. He had less time for relaxed work, but did achieve a small number of gem-like canvases, unstrained, wholesome, and filled with a yearning for happiness, which was scarce in his life by this stage.*

Oil on paper (on board); 50.8 x 60.9 cm
National Gallery of Ireland

PLATE 9

Marshall Foch 1918

Pl 9 **T**he French general of the First World War was an outstanding figure, greatly admired by Orpen, and painted by him in an unheroic, relaxed and altogether human way. It was Orpen's job to paint portraits, and when he went to war as an official war artist in 1916 he transferred this skill to the fighting man.

23

Oil on canvas; 91.4 x 76.2 cm
Imperial War Museum, London

PLATE 10

Resting 1905

24

Pl 10   This is one of Orpen's great works from the period *1905–8, when he used as his model Lottie Stafford, a washerwoman from Chelsea. She had a wonderful 'swan-neck' which greatly appealed to Orpen, and which he emphasised in his paintings.*

Oil on canvas; 76.2 x 55.8 cm
Ulster Museum, Belfast

cont. from p12

public houses which Victorian artists had made famous.

Orpen mirrored the period in his works, as well as reflecting a mercurial response to the great exhibitions of Watteau, Rembrandt, Chardin and Velázquez. His versatility was immense. He could 'take off' a style or a gesture in other painters, absorb the essence, and throw away any latent dependency, so that, though one sees the powerful influence in his early work of world masters, it is never *25* plagiarism. Instead, he pays them the supreme tribute of absorbing and revitalising their greatest skills.

To this period, from 1900 to about 1906, belong a succession of his masterpieces, in which the influences particularly of Velázquez, whose work he saw on a trip to Madrid with Hugh Lane, are apparent. Orpen was lucky also to have as model Lottie Stafford, a striking Junoesque figure. She features in his paintings *The Wash House* (*Pl 4*), *Resting* (*Pl 10*), and *Lottie of Paradise Walk* (Leeds City Art Gallery).

During the same period, Orpen produced a number of fine self-portraits. He had used his own face as subject matter in his art, despite having grave reservations about the attractiveness of his appearance. He made a joke about this, and claimed that the reservation had been there since his extreme youth. Yet photographs do not bear out his argument, and it seems more likely that it was an attitude adopted deliberately by Orpen, who was in fact very attractive. Among the self-portraits is an accomplished oil sketch, in the Ashmolean Museum, Oxford, showing him at the age of thirteen, and there are several studies of him from the Slade School period. Self-portraiture for Orpen fulfilled a very complex and deep personal need; essentially inarticulate in expressing matters relating to his spiritual and creative nature—though he was highly articulate and witty at the level of lighter issues—Orpen studied himself in order to understand what art was about, which direction he should be taking with his life, and what point of achievement he had reached at any of the frequent occasions of such self-analysis. The many self-portraits throughout his career, several of which represent outstanding drawings, watercolours and paintings in twentieth-century art, are in part puzzled examinations of his nature and purpose. They represent a kind of visual 'diary', the pouring forth, in pencil, wash or oil-paint, of himself.

The intensity of these works was translated by Orpen into the main occupation of his early years, and of his later career—professional portraiture. This was to develop into a highly accomplished and extremely lucrative full-time practice, well before the outbreak of the First World War. But in its early stages he found the work difficult, and struggled to provide for himself and his family by travelling around the country to complete portrait commissions. He found children particularly difficult; but he increasingly impressed his adult clients, notably women, and he developed a skill which led to such splendid and lasting monuments of his art as the portrait of James Staats Forbes (Manchester City Art Gallery), Augustus John (National Portrait Gallery), Herbert Everett (Imperial War Museum), George Moore (Private Collection), Lord Iveagh (Private Collection), and the series done for Hugh Lane in Dublin. These included Tim Healy, Michael Davitt, William O'Brien and John Pentland Mahaffy.

Orpen's nudes, during the first ten years of his working life, are stunningly beautiful. They are also daring, in the pose, in the frankness of his composition, and in the extent to which he always treated the female form as a human character. He never simply paints flesh, or a pretty figure. The anguish and feeling of the character are ever-present. He regarded the accomplishment as enormously difficult, and wrote on one occasion to William Rothenstein, an older friend and artist who took a similar direction towards portrait-painting, that nothing was as difficult as the nude, and that many of the greatest nude paintings failed in one way or another. But his *A Woman (Pl 5)* and *A Spanish Woman* (both Leeds), though totally different from each other, demonstrate the breadth of his vision and the technical capacity to 'bring off' this difficult kind of picture.

A final group of works to be considered is that embracing the domestic pictures, which represented a substantial output during the formative years. Orpen married early. His wife Grace was from an artistic family, the Knewstubs;

her sister was married to William Rothenstein, and her brother ran a gallery in Chelsea. Their first child, Mary, was born in 1902, and their second daughter, Kit, in 1906, and the domestic scene was happy, if turbulent. Many portraits of Grace Knewstub were painted during these years, as well as drawings and paintings of the children. From this work Orpen developed a new kind of portraiture, that of family groups, and he produced a number, the most famous being *A Bloomsbury Family*, which shows the Nicholsons, two of whom, William the father, and Ben, were painters.

Orpen recognised that success and fortune, in the old-fashioned sense, lay for him in England. His life and practice were centred there. His standards conformed to British requirements. He knew, in a word, on which side his bread was buttered. Yet he was, at heart, an Irishman, wayward and rebellious, and he stood outside the throng of English art in the early years of the century, keeping his counsel, painting well, and escaping across the Irish Sea whenever he could.

It created a slightly schizophrenic character, with Orpen the Irishman turning himself into a stage Irishman, painting himself as a man of the west, and emphasising the Irish accent when in the company of English people. But he also played the successful English professional, and maintained a high standard of living. He was never ostentatious, and he was always generous. Though he loved to drink champagne at lunchtime, and could easily afford to do so,

he used to have it served in a pewter beer tankard so as not to embarrass his friends, who could not afford to drink with the same extravagance.

The opportunity to escape home to Ireland regularly came in the early days. His abilities were quickly and widely recognised, and he was offered a teaching post at the Metropolitan School of Art in Dublin in 1902; for the following fifteen years he became the dominant artist teaching there, setting the school's standards in painting and at the same time making a huge impact on artistic life in the city generally. He exhibited in Dublin. He became an associate of the Royal Hibernian Academy, and then a full academician. He developed a dual portrait practice, with a growing list of sitters on both sides of the Irish Sea. If all things had been equal, he would undoubtedly have preferred Ireland to England.

He liberated art in Ireland. He introduced proper life classes, bringing in from England professional female models who posed in the nude, and allowed the proper teaching of life painting. Before, when he had been a student, prudery surrounded the painting of the nude, and embarrassment prevailed at every turn. He changed all that, giving to generations of Irish artists a confidence and a relaxed approach to their work which has lasted ever since.

Perhaps he wanted monetary success too much, just as he wanted critical recognition. A former student, Theodosia Townshend, said of his search for fame and his desire to be a Royal Academician: 'It was rather shaming when Orpen began to exhibit with the Royal Academy. Rather like knowing Nixon. He wouldn't talk to me about it. I would have exuded disapproval'; and of his desire for money, she simply dismissed it as an inappropriate endorsement of success.

30

❧

THE WAR YEARS AND AFTER

The First World War provided a great challenge for Orpen. At the time his studio assistant was Seán Keating. Well before 1916 Keating saw the war as creating a dividing line between Britain and Ireland. He urged Orpen to choose his own country, to return there, and make a life for himself away from the growing pressures of a society portrait practice which was already placing strains on his marriage and art. But Orpen chose differently. They parted company. Keating returned home, became a teacher at the Metropolitan School, and was a major influence on Irish art from then on. Orpen tried briefly to experiment with new techniques of painting and new ideas in composition, and produced major canvases such as *The Holy Well* (National Gallery of Ireland). But his day-to-day burden was

the commissioned portrait, which he did superbly—it paid him handsomely into the bargain. He lived well, drove a Rolls Royce, had an enduring love affair with Mrs St George, and pursued an existence increasingly separate from his wife and family.

The war forced him into a period of self-analysis, and led him to become an official war artist, and to go off to the Western Front in the spring of 1916. There, he attempted to paint the war as comprehensively as possible. He continued, without ceasing, until the conclusion of the Peace Conference in 1920, and he produced arguably the greatest body of war art history has known, exceeding the output of such painters as Goya, who pursued the same objective during the Napoleonic campaigns in Spain, or Jacques Callot, who did the same during the Thirty Years War in the seventeenth century.

Orpen could be riotously funny, and was often engaged in leg-pulling episodes, one of the more outrageous being his creation of a completely mythical story about a famous woman spy who was arrested and tried. When she came to be executed she appeared before the firing squad wearing an army greatcoat, which she shrugged off just before the order to fire was given, and she was of course wearing nothing underneath. Orpen allegedly painted her portrait—in fact it was the portrait of his mistress, Yvonne Aubicq—and presented the whole story to the War Information Department as fact. It was believed and widely reported, and when the truth was discovered, Orpen got into trouble. But he had friends in high places, including Field Marshall Lord Haig, and he got off with a mild reprimand.

A vast array of Orpen's canvases, drawings and water-colours depict the plight of the fighting man, the mangled aftermath of strife, the horrors of the battlefield itself, the poignancy of human bewilderment and fear, even the courage. Orpen came to hate and despise the politicians who had caused so much carnage. And his visual comments at the end take on an almost daemonic fury against war and its skilled practitioners. He employs parody, satire, irony and disdain to humiliate and belittle the ogres of war, and he uses his limpid colours and his clear line to augment and memorialise the achievements of the fighting man, who became heroic in Orpen's eyes.

The First World War and its grim aftermath left Orpen sick, exhausted, and disgusted. He had turned to drink during the period of the war, to alleviate some of the distress. He had also met a most beautiful blonde Belgian model, Yvonne Aubicq, with whom he lived during the 1920s in Paris, and who joined him in his pursuit of pleasure and excitement in the giddy aftermath of those cataclysmic years. His life revolved around the racecourse, the bar, the club, motoring to Dieppe, to the south of France, to Deauville. And to fund this, he took on more and more of the smart portrait commissions for which his

style was eminently suited.

He returned to Ireland after the war for one day only, in 1918. And though he professed love for the country, which in a nostalgic sense was genuine enough, his interpretation of being Irish became a sentimental one. He had transformed himself into a world figure, an artist earning phenomenal sums of money and spending it with prodigious energy and enthusiasm.

33

By the mid-1920s he was burnt out. His portraiture became somewhat automatic, though technically it remained skilled and impressive. He separated himself from his wife and children; because of the ravages of drink, he could not bear it when his daughter Kit called to see him, and he had his servants turn her away from the door. He was deserted by his friends, and sponged on by unworthy acquaintances. He had the generosity of spirit to persuade Yvonne to leave him, and she married his chauffeur, Charles Grover Williams, who later became a racing driver, and still later a worker for the French Resistance in the Second World War, before being captured and tortured to death by the Nazis.

Orpen published two books during the last decade of his life: a memoir of his early life, *Stories of Old Ireland and Myself*, and a memoir of the First World War, *An Onlooker in France*. Both demonstrate, often through their very simplicity and emotionalism, the complexity of his character.

Orpen made a profound contribution to art in this century. He was decidedly unfashionable in despising the very idea of artists conforming to a required mode of painting. He was an unparalleled draughtsman, and his drawings stand with the best of any century. He was a sensitive and sympathetic portraitist, though he might have endeared himself more to posterity if he had leavened the portrait commissions with more genre paintings and more nudes. The limited number of nudes he painted are among his greatest works.

His teacher, Henry Tonks, argued after Orpen's death that he somehow missed his mark as a result of his pursuit of the portrait commission. Works that have come to light in the last ten or so years fundamentally disprove this view, and demonstrate repeatedly the range and profundity of his artistic perception. Consistently, in recent years, his reputation has risen, from a grudging acceptance of his ability to paint and his impact as a teacher, to the more profound belief that he stands as an artist worthy of world recognition. He is not the only Irish artist to occupy such a place. But, it can be argued, he is the most influential upon his own time, and upon the generations which followed him.

34